In Pilgrim Drag

poems by

Susan M. G. Dingle

Finishing Line Press
Georgetown, Kentucky

In Pilgrim Drag

For David

Copyright © 2020 by Susan M. G. Dingle
ISBN 978-1-64662-292-4 First Edition
All rights reserved under International and Pan-American Copyright Conventions. No part of this book may be reproduced in any manner whatsoever without written permission from the publisher, except in the case of brief quotations embodied in critical articles and reviews.

ACKNOWLEDGMENTS

"Listening to the Names" in *Fifth Wednesday Journal*, Spring 2017, Issue 20
"Big Sister in the Promised Land" in *Poets to Come*. Local Gems, 2019
"Monday in February" in *Leaves of Me*, edited by Gladys Henderson and Peter Dugan. 2019
"An Explanation," in *Bards Annual 2019*

Publisher: Leah Maines
Editor: Christen Kincaid
Cover Art and Design: Mick Wieland
Author Photo: Thomas Kochie

Order online: www.finishinglinepress.com
also available on amazon.com

Author inquiries and mail orders:
Finishing Line Press
P. O. Box 1626
Georgetown, Kentucky 40324
U. S. A.

Table of Contents

August in the Greenport Hospital 1
An Explanation 2
The Christmas We Had 5
Psalm 1 6

Restoration 7
Listening to the Names 8
Cliff Notes 9
At The Parrish 11
14 Ways of Seeing Being White 12
Prophecy 16
After the Apocalypse 17
Big Sister in the Promised Land 18

Graveyard of the Atlantic 19
In Pilgrim Drag 20
During Hurricane Season 21
Signs & Wonders 22
Where the Pilgrims Almost Landed 23

An American Psalmist 24

Googling Zion 28
Psalm with No Apology 29
Monday in February 30
How A Girl Becomes a Warrior 31

August in the Greenport Hospital

In the ER Tuesday night,
the nurse inserts a needle you hardly feel,
and draws five tubes of blood
before you know it.

In the next bed, knees
point beneath a sheet,
a skeleton draped with flesh,
whose bony head lifts in our direction,
an aged woman, her eyes bright,
beneath a monitor tracking heart rate and oxygen.

I pull the faded curtains along a track
around your bed and my chair
as if we might find privacy,

when still we hear the monitor beep
and a thin voice answer,
"Hello? Hello?"
like a cat crying at a door,

"Hello? Hello?"

I ask the nurse to turn off the monitor.
But she says the woman's over ninety,
a DNR.

We never had dinner.
By the time I go out for pizza,
and come back with root beer,

the other cubicle is empty, the monitor is gone.

We can't remember
the last time we had root beer.

An Explanation

The reason it seems like the world is falling apart
is because it really is,
just look at that desk.
The souvenir fairies from Ireland, gift from your granddaughter,
still in cellophane, next to the textbook
of Alcoholics Anonymous on top of
new and selected poems that explain about God,
the timesheet for the caregivers whose shifts
begin today, after the Primary Care
Physician said you are failing.

You disagree. You think there is a new injection
the doctor doesn't know about. In your sleep you explain.

I catalog what is falling apart. So far
I didn't even finish
the desk but at least the handmade wooden manger scene
is in order, the interlocking pieces
grooved together, hooves of the camel

on top of the hooves of the lamb, and human
curves stacking neatly around them.

It took me twenty minutes to put it back together,
without the diagram I couldn't find
until I didn't need it any more.

ii
No one starts out being a hoarder.
It's just when you lose so much,
you can't let anything go,
old Christmas cards returned in the mail
from people who are probably dead
or moved, you can't keep up

Canvas bags stuffed with magazines whose unread
articles might matter someday;
papers I don't know where to file,

a souvenir bottle in the shape of a maple leaf
filled with syrup, from a wedding in Vermont
(the handmade tag says "Thank You,")

a heart constructed of Legos by a granddaughter several years ago,
and a plastic dog the size of a fingertip another granddaughter
gave me as I was leaving,
"something to remember her by."

I dream of clear surfaces,
where all the old clothes are given away
and a homeless woman enjoys
sewing on the button for that thick cable knit
I no longer wear.

iii
God is good, forever giving us things to do
when we think we should be doing
other things, for example
paying bills right now,
especially the electric, three months overdue, because you
always paid them, your ledgers now illegible,
handwriting cramped into hieroglyph
letters like ibis scratching across Egypt.

I am color-coding folders,
red is for Home Care, green is for
Caregiver Schedules, purple is for Poems (Current)
I don't care if it's bad luck.

On the desk I find a yellow plastic
tape measure labeled "For help with blindness,
please call National Federation for the blind."

iv
Anything made of cloth
can be folded and placed in a pile.
Then the pile can be moved to another room.

v
I wish I knew what to do with books I haven't read
or how to repair the nightstand that shattered
the last time you fell.

The Christmas We Had

was not the one we expected.

We heard a song, "once in Royal David's City,"
in a solo voice, treble,

joined by alto, tenor, baritone, bass, a full choir for the second verse,
"He came down to earth from heaven."

Our guests leave early Christmas day,
before you throw up.
I hold the mixing bowl
beneath your chin, wipe your mouth with Kleenex.

Christmas eve at the family service
the Pastor and I perform a dialogue between an unborn spirit
(him) and an angel (me), explaining what he might expect
in human life, him not entirely convinced
birth would be worth it,

but you couldn't hear us from the second row.

After you throw up and say you are okay,
I ask would you like to hear the Christmas Eve dialogue again
and you say yes, so I read both the unborn and the angel,

& you look at me as if you can hear it,
at least somewhat, but anyway you are happy, that I can see.

The rest of the day you slept, in the kitchen the Lord was with me.

Psalm 1

O Lord, I write for your eyes only.

In the middle of the night I wake up with dread so familiar it
                               might as well have its own website
"darknightofthesoul.com,"
                 where unheeded warnings haunt the home page,
     graffiti left by suicides,
                     evidence the infrastructure might give way
if synapses disintegrate—

I read about the earthquake in Katmandu
 where antique lattice topples balconies and ornate wooden windows
                 clatter Sunday morning,
shatter little shrines nested in the crooks of old houses,
                           all buckle into dust cloud
when Kali shakes her garland of skulls
                     and skirt of dismembered arms
        "having liberated Her children from attachment to the body,"

the spirit bell quivers in the aftershocks.

                     Still indigenous people return,
          show up and kneel there,

pile up their flower petals, wave their beads, worship in the rubble

       of the sacred site.
                    Where else might they go?

Children drawing pictures of God, depict God smiling,
     as if they feel His kindness, His presence.

                 Birds outside my window
stir and brighten.
       I hear you turn sorrow
    into dancing.
             I wait for your reply.

Restoration

1.
We will overcome every trauma:
My teacher wrote the book.

Protective factors include optimism and faith.

82% of people encounter trauma.
Some stressors might be intergenerational
or culturally based.

Damages require tools.

2.
The conservator
places the drawing
in water so absent of acid
it's almost dry.

If I were that drawing,
I would float beneath the light,
grape leaves shining.

Destruction doesn't always win,
Look for clues you did survive.

3.
If I am to be restored,
I must be perfectly honest.

Pinchers lift me to a table.
I lie beneath wood blocks.
I see the fibers, Japanese paper
winnowed down to a single cell

placed by a tweezer,
smoothed by the slurry
from a hypodermic

where the wound began,
it reaches me.

Listening to the Names

15 years later it is the first time
you sit there
at the kitchen table,
a lotus

listening to voices
pronounce each syllable
correctly,

see a face with each name,
an age and place of origin

you have been,
Monmouth, Little Silver,
Ronkonkoma,

some readers not yet born
that morning

there was no water
rising and falling,

no silver bell,

no white roses, red roses,
little flags
stuck between letters,

no black granite
carved with names.

Cliff Notes

Foster diversity. Don't label and stereotype others.
                                        (Such a transgender wannabe!)

While the psychological condition became known as "Stockholm Syndrome"
        due to the publicity, the emotional "bonding" with captors was a
        familiar story recognized in studies of hostage, prisoner or abusive
        situations

                      I write in pencil so I can erase myself.

      Approach each interaction with respect, regardless of whether you
believe the other person's behaviors deserve respect.

      You look like a god, he said, lying.
                      Anything that does not look like a poem
I will erase.
          Tied to a chair,
                      I invent my own algorithm.
Listen without interrupting.
                      I am not a god, I am tied to a chair.

      Be a bridge builder. Create an inclusive environment,
an algorithm tied to your fingers, a pencil, a geography of metaphor and/or
      injustice.

                  Ask yourself questions like
        How will I look back on these circumstances,
                      unearthed ruins,
strike-outs, errors, lifetime advantages including color.

Don't look at me like that.

Peroxide froths on blood, heats up, removes every stain:
        this is why girls going to proms still dress like drag queens,
                          manage reactions

and respond in an appropriate manner, a positive and solution-driven
        approach.
                  We bleed in pencil,
Practice self-restraint. Focus on

    the names of untold innocents, survivors, and family members
of Freddie Grey, Tamir Rice, Trayvon Martin,
an alphabet of grief—
                      blood-soaked cell phone, child in back seat,
mother live streaming,
                                      pencil shrieks neon.

Postscript: *Facebook, November 6, 2016*

My dog, Miss Lili, had what was called "global anxiety."
One person I know says I am heartless. Please don't judge other pet owners.
Most are doing the best they can.

Language Sources: Stanislaus County Office of Education, "Choose Civility Principles;" Web MD, "Stockholm Syndrome," Facebook posting, James Tate

At the Parrish

After a painting by Jane Freilicher

Anemones
                                           float above the water
                reflecting in a mirror,

                        a face so white,
I only see Watermill.

                                           I never noticed
                when the sun is shining, how invisible
my skin is
           as long as everyone else's skin is
                                  also white
I don't
        say anything about color

                        but I can't help noticing
not one brown face in this museum,
         whose white walls extend to
                  a window, the horizon
echoes an empty field after a harvest,

                & the Shinnecock selling cigarettes
at the edge of the Res, smoke shops
                    I do not see.

14 Ways of Seeing Being White

*A Reflection upon reading Citizen. An American Lyric
by Claudia Rankine*

1.
I am a perpetrator
of history
imagining I am blameless:

no physical evidence
connects me
with these crimes

but my denial of
the vast white conspiracy.

If I accuse myself,
I am lying

2.
I can't remember
the name of my college roommate
only that she never spoke to me
after I expressed some sympathy
over how difficult it must be for her
being black at a school so white

her friends didn't speak to me either
after that
& it took me
fifty years later
to figure out why.

3.
The only time I have to think about race
is when something happens on television,
another black man killed by police
for no reason.
The rest of the time

I don't have to.

4.
Now I am saying
what you already know,
if you are a person of color reading this.
It is like looking under a rock,
you see what squirms.

5.
People who look like me
are saying,
she's crazy.

6.
When white people talk about black people,
why do "we" lower "our" voices,
as if "they" might be listening?
Some white people I know
also lower their voices when they talk about someone who is
(Jewish).
I always want to speak up and say
Speak up!
But so far I haven't.

7.
In poetry is sanctuary
for things I cannot say.
In Riverhead they told the Reverend
there was no racism in Riverhead
until he showed up
and started talking about it.

8.
Anything we don't talk about

doesn't exist.

9.
I feel my nerve endings through my sweater.

10.
Another bold and meaningless claim
from someone who sat at dinner parties
at the 21 Club while other white people
told racist jokes
and didn't say anything.

11.
Of course I have white guilt
and of course it is meaningless:
when Jesus forgave sins
he did not say, go and continue sinning,
he said go and sin no more.

What would it mean if a white person
renounced the sin of racism
and really meant it, what
would that even look like.

12.
A lie. It would look like a lie.
When the well is poisoned,
every drop is tainted.

13.
Everything I am saying
is driven by a truth beneath the lie,
that much I do know.

14.
What if Philip Pettit had been a black man
and went wire-walking
between the North and South Towers,
what do you think the white police
who stood at both corners
and watched him
stepping over the void,
balancing and turning around
on the high wire,
resisting arrest,
would have done?

Prophecy

He stalks you like a jaguar,
the lord of the underworld native Americans call
"he who kills with one leap,"
but you don't recognize a jaguar when you see one:
You imagine he will deliver you
with razzle-dazzle at rallies, tweeting coded messages.

I see how he grooms you,
lures you with rumors and innuendo,
pretending to be your friend—
But you do not know how patient evil can be.

One day he will mount you, an insect pinned on velvet,
a butterfly glittering with regret, yearning for chloroform,
and you won't report it, but I am the witness,
once victim, now accuser: I speak in your name.

After the Apocalypse

Leaf-glitter litters down a gold road,
                                  branches ache a broke sky

(you can make $100 a day on your computer
by sending out links on a private server
                      for a onetime fee of only $97 if you act now:

consider this offer.)

                  Gold veins rain down,
grackles hop dry stalks. We have so little time,
                  too old to know any better, too gone to find
the bottom line scrolling down the phone,
                  looking for what was lost a generation ago,

like the divorced mom with two kids and no skills who became a millionaire
              in just 15 minutes a day, as recommended by

this guy from Shark Tank you're sure would never lie.
        He's a billionaire, you say, why would he lie?

After the Apocalypse down-trodden leaves
                          soar toward their lost branches,
glittery music of morning, keening lost
        victories like armloads of clothes in an agitating cycle,
gold blades bursting the canopy,
                        millions of stillborn leaves flying home,
"Hosanna," they whisper, what could happen
   if you press this green button at the end of the screen: "act now."

After the Apocalypse, this offer will not be recognized.

Big Sister in the Promised Land

Bring me your broken stuff. I will hand out slick prayers and wristbands.
I drive into a tree at 90 mph and walk away. I am made of steel

densely packed as any molecule on the surface of Mars.
People look at me like I'm crazy. I hand out leaflets on how to be grateful.

I took the laundry down to the washer, set it on fire, then call 911.
It is embarrassing when dinner guests ask what happened to the tablecloth.

I know you didn't mean it. It was all my fault I did not see the silver lining.
You are always so positive, like when the wind blew the roof off the house
and you say

now we can see the stars. I said in a hurricane there are no stars. Now
I am sorry
I stole your dream and instead you got diabetes. You were so hooked on

sugar, you kept a refrigerator in the living room, you couldn't
throw anything away,
two of us patched together with bleeding prayers.

At last I tell the truth and it will set you free,
but it is too broken to make any sense.
When the language betrayed us, this is how I cry,
this is what it looks like

after 40 years in the desert when you see the promised land.

Graveyard of the Atlantic

Yesterday three or four seals, maybe two,
                         raise their dark heads and look at me
before they dive away
                               but today the tide's gone out,
I do not see them.
                  Did the sharks find them,
the sharks I didn't see

                                    evidence of slaughter
                hidden in the tide
so far away the waves shake out their handkerchiefs,

as if they come to say goodbye:
        I can no longer wait in the sun for the tide's return
when the bright sea blisters and burns, the victims hidden.

In Pilgrim Drag

Ribbons in rainbow colors strung between trees,
        handwritten messages for those who died of AIDS,
now raised up above the stage, a shimmery festoon for a tall drag queen
        in towering silver crown and gloves
who gestures a sign of peace,
                as a town crier in pilgrim drag belts out
"I know a land where dreams are born"
        in counterpoint to her "someday I'll wish upon a star."

Heroes of the culture war wear drag to victory
        though transgender soldiers are prohibited from service—
we stand together disenfranchised,
    Muslims, children of the undocumented, those whose taxes rise
               as their health care diminishes, black people
disproportionately slain by police, people of color
                with whom we mark
these festivities of grief.

During Hurricane Season

A Jamaican woman in the fish market says one storm passed over Jamaica
        and two more are coming,
                "in the end times this is what you expect."

In the end times maybe God means me to travel to this mountain
        that isn't a mountain, it's sand dunes
between the dune shacks and the sea, transcribing messages

        the 75 year old singer at the piano bar drinks club soda and tells stories about
Carol Channing falling asleep in the cabaret until as he vamps out the intro to "Hello Dolly,"

        and she awakens, his homage to Marilyn Monroe and all those queens of yesterday
who still cruise Commercial Street, do you remember Stonewall?

        Torch singer under a spotlight he turns on himself like a flashlight,
his broad voice and bald head beaming,

 he belts out "I wanna be loved by you," looking out over the tip jar for that affirming glance,
    like it's 1985, and whoever he once loved still stands a chance.

Signs & Wonders

> *No one knows*
> *I am gay.*
> *T-Shirt in A Window, Provincetown 2017*

I don't know
                        how long I've been sitting here
            but sun has moved way up in the sky and now the shadow
of my pencil is neon, my hand is on fire
                a neon sign.

Where the Pilgrims Almost Landed

                I lay on a blanket in the sand all day,
human sacrifice on an altar of seashells, white girl seeking the perfect tan
rather than the burn that blisters into cancer decades later,

      who needs L.A. when you have Provincetown and the dunes

for pilgrimage: the pilgrims knew, which is why they landed here
            under a canvas canopy I'm half a couple
from a wedding cake, the female equivalent of a drag queen in an imaginary
      t-shirt,
possible transgender wannabe,
                  neither straight nor gay,
the perfect anomaly.
            Trauma will do that for you, so be a good sport,
bless every dune shack
     standing on holy ground where the graveyard of the Atlantic
meets the smell of bacon frying in a pan,
        green tea, barefoot, you and me
                 interpreting the shadows of a canopy,
the holy ground,
   an accordion with pleats of land and clumps between, a shack,
         a shed among outcroppings,

a shore where the pilgrims almost landed, but decided the soil was too rocky
and the tide drop so crazy they drafted the Mayflower Compact
         and never came ashore here, but at Plymouth instead.

Despite the enslavement of Africans and genocide of First People,
we claim God's grace.
              Finally we come ashore
                   in a world where people can love whoever they want to.

On the Provincetown ferry, the conductor calls, "Watch your ears,"
            before the Long Point fog horn blasts us home.

An American Psalmist

1.
When saddled horses were led to the very sanctuary of the temple, Haggai Sophia, some of these, unable to keep their footing on the splendid and slippery pavement, were stabbed when they fell, so that the sacred pavement was polluted with blood and filth[1]

                              My mother died
when it was too late to cancel the trip
                                        so we're in Athens
for the baptism of a granddaughter

            when the second tower fell and we see it on Greek TV,
the second tower fell with voiceover narration we don't understand until we
find the BBC the second tower fell.

We fly to Istanbul because the trip is planned,
                     a Turkish barge one morning on the Bosporus
   I bang my head on a wooden beam, between Europe and Asia
when they ask if I am American, I say I am from New York

I don't feel anything

            My mother died when it was too late to cancel the trip
We visit Haggai Sophia, the Blue Mosque once a cathedral but we didn't know
about it
           I see seraphim within the dome
                     concealed inside gold flames, Arabic calligraphy

2.
For the sacred altar, formed of all kinds of precious metals and admired by the whole world, was broken into bits and distributed among the soldiers…

After the linden tree by the kitchen door is cut down and the stump ground up,
                           my mother plants succulents to cover
the blank space I was weeding that morning she died anyway. I was so surprised,

I thought she would live forever.

3.
When [the contents of Haggai Sophia] were to be borne away, mules and saddled horses led to the very sanctuary of the temple, the most heinous sins and crimes committed by all with equal zeal²

    Haggai Sophia, the great church of Holy Wisdom,
        dome of the sepulchral Virgin
in whose vault an altar floats, images of saints appear,
       pentimento,
a mother who when you cry in the night toughens you up by not answering,
        a mother who cries in the night, not answered.

4.
Nothing was more difficult and laborious than to soften by prayers, to render benevolent, these wrathful barbarians, often they drew their daggers against anyone who opposed them at all, no one was without a share in the grief³

around the dome the script of hammered gold curlicues like leaping flames,

strands of light, trails of planes across the sky

    *40 windows with sunlight coming through the cupola
irradiating its gold mosaics, seem to dissolve the solidity of the walls"*⁴

      the dome at the center between two half domes
four pendentives into
        the square shape of its piers below
the weight of the dome to the walls balance of brick and mortar
          under it, a vault with its

supporting arches a curved triangle balanced by the intersection of a dome,
        icons painted over,
mosaic tiles being restored,
        a tower of cast iron scaffolding
patches of moisture and peeling paint; bricked-up windows;
      marble panels…obscured under layers of grime;
walls covered in mustard-colored paint after golden mosaics had fallen away.⁵

5.
In the alleys, in the streets, in the temples, complaints, weeping, lamentations, grief, the groaning of men, the shrieks of women, wounds, rape, captivity, the separation of those most closely united...[6]

I don't ask because you won't answer,

                                                I am only a tourist,
      a New Yorker, I don't live here so I can't ask and
                      you can't tell me
anyway your language makes no sense to me
                centuries before blood pours out, on this floor,

beneath this dome,
                      this cobbled span
once the slaughterhouse of the 4th Crusade,
                an ocean churned inside out, upside down,

these tentacles of light from the dome above,
                                pentimento between gold flames,
     prophecies we cannot read,
injuries we cannot heal.

Hooves clatter on the threshing floor,
                    clobber blood, soak into cobblestone

       this Blue Mosque whose seraphim explain
                        nothing I can do but praise you

even as you take it all away

6.
I didn't know Istanbul was once Byzantium, before that Constantinople,

                    the Blue Mosque
a prayer left standing,
       phantom cathedral, museum of cast iron scaffolding
and ephemeral sunlight where we hold hands and looked up,
            in the tenth year of our marriage

on the 13th of September the month after my mother died, two days
        after September 11, I was so numb as even now as he declines

I praise you, dear Creator, even as you take this life away.
        Your word says you will turn sorrow into dancing,
but not how or when, not that I'm asking, I praise you anyway.

---

[1] Nicetas Choniates on the Sack of Constantinople, 1204, reprinted in Coakley, John W. and Sterk, Andrea. Readings in World Christian History, Volume I: Earliest Christianity to 1453, p. 336. Orbis Books: Maryknoll, NY 2016.
[2] Ibid.
[3] Ibid.
[4] Victoria Hammond," Visions of Heaven: The Dome in European Architecture" (Springer, 2005).
[5] https://www.smithsonianmag.com/travel/a-monumental-struggle-to-preserve-hagia-sophia-92038218/#UucdCu3FXFudK4dV.99
[6] Nicetas Choniates, in Coakley & Sterk, Op. cit.

Googling Zion

> *"By the waters of Babylon, there we sat down and wept,
> when we remembered Zion"*   —Psalm 137:1

While we are driving, you ask what "Zion" means,
       this name so common out here, a church, a town, a bowling alley
       where redwoods pierce the sky on the mountain
       across from Mt. Hood in the Pacific Northwest where you live,

      your son in the backseat listening as we drive to his ball game,

and I promise I will google it but I forget
       until this morning on the East End by the Peconic Bay,
I google "Zion,"

   "a small mountain in Jerusalem where the ark of the covenant was placed."

    "the hill of Jerusalem on which the city of David was built,"

God's dwelling place.

              If only the history of Zion were that simple,
although at the Mt. Zion Bowling alley in southern Washington it is easy
                  to rent shoes and bowl a frame or two

where the ark of the covenant is placed
                           so if you want to find it
you have to go there,

wherever the blessed covenant
        dwells sacred and apart, yet always with you:

Zion,
     the mound where your son stands to pitch for the first time

and two generations watch from behind home plate.

Psalm with No Apology

*For the congregation of the Shinnecock Presbyterian Church,
October 21, 2018*

This morning the big field is vacant
                            sets of metal bleachers face each other
                    uninhabited, two empty cars on the far side,
a sign that says SLOW DOWN.

                It is October, the slow time between seasons,
when reverence is all I bring,
                    for the elders who meet on Wed. at 6 PM,
                    for the driver of the vehicle
who tails an unfamiliar car on this road toward the burial ground:

                    I do not know who the ancestors were
who trod this field, the generations
                        who worship here
          between seasons, after the pow-wow
                        this morning I speak from the pulpit
              to native people who have invited me, beloved community
who pray for children, suffer from substance abuse, violence and trauma,
outsiders who were here first, that we may witness
and find refuge in this broken land,
                      where grandmothers in the back pews

      still offer stubborn prayers.

Monday in February

I walk where the water is frozen—
under ice, waves don't break, but slush
dark in open spaces between slashes of snow,
ice crust piled up like waves frozen while breaking.

I want to walk on the ice out to the depths where open water glitters

but too much weight would break the ice
and I would drown looking back
on this beach so desolate only the compassion of God can melt it,

"fight, flight or freeze" being the only choices in extreme circumstances
such as Monday in February, hearing of another death,

I keep walking even though all I see is frozen,
that shock of molten blue at the horizon, dark ice slushing at my feet.

Up the beach I find a box of matches,
wooden sticks with green tops in neat rows,
but no flint so I can't light one.
I take home an unseen light.

How a Girl Becomes a Warrior

1.

The week after the first woman is nominated
to be President of the United States,
94 years after women won the right to vote,
I remember women with bound feet, their ideal
a geisha prancing on tiptoe, toes broken, crushed into claws
from the age of five when the binding begins,
enveloped in embroidery.

My mother strides to the office in stilettos,
a career that ends in marriage and misshapen feet,
a husband deciding she should stay home.

When I was ten, I want to argue in court like Perry Mason on TV,
but girls can't be lawyers. Outside I practice
pitching and fielding but girls can't play in the majors.

Girls can be teachers, nurses, secretaries,
Mothers, movie stars or strippers.
Girls must be pretty and thin.

Some girls don't buy in.

2.

The week after the first woman is nominated to be President
94 years after women won the right to vote,
I see you on a screen, a girl
of sixteen wearing a yellow lace dress and sparkly blue flats.
You say your name is Memory Banda
and you are from Malawi.

You say you are not getting married
until you want to. You tell about the camp in Malawi
where young girls are forced into "sexual cleansing" to rid them
of "childhood dust," those motes of fantasy and curiosity about the world

that swirl in sunlight toward a future exterminated
in a ceremony called "Kusasa Fumbi," like ethnic cleansing
only with sex instead of machetes, leaving many little girls impregnated
or infected, and all girls abandoned and shamed.

You, Memory, refuse to go to the camp though women in your village
say you are stupid to want to go to school, have a career.
You say, why can't I change something?

3.

You say, I will be a warrior,
gather the girls in your village, help them remember
how to read, and together you text the traditional leaders
incessantly to pass a new law in the Parliament of Malawi
raising the age of marriage to 18.

Warriors always have more to do.
Today you smile, remind grownups we must enforce the law.

I am old, Memory, but when I hear you say
*We are not just women, we are not just girls, we are
extraordinary,* I believe you.

The week after the first woman is nominated to be President
94 years after women won the right to vote.

Additional Acknowledgements

Thank you, Jake and Natalie, and Chloe, Taylor, Coby, Tanner, Myradie and Lucie. Thank you to Michael, Leslie, Jeffrey, Christopher, Mark and Liz, and the extended Dingle family. Thank you to Avis Lemard and Larry Behr, our support team.

Thank you to my friends from Baltimore Friends, especially Savitri, Suzy, Kathy, Marianne & Peter, Greg, Paul, Annie, Betsy & Lee, Joe & Ozzie.

Thank you to Poetry Street, especially Bubbie, Maggie, and Chip Williford, Gladys Henderson, Diana Turesi, Nina Yavel, and Steve Kramer.

Thank you to Julie Sheehan and fellow students Tyler Allen Perry, Caroline DeLuca, Miranda Beeson, Julie Scarr, Lily Wann and Anthony DiPietro in the "Powers of Poetry" graduate seminar, Fall 2016, in the SUNY Stony Brook/Southampton MFA program.

Thank you to Rev. Charles A. Coverdale, Rev. Cynthia Liggon, Rev. Montez Johnson, Prophet F.W. Hood and First Baptist Church of Riverhead; Rev. Natalie Wimberly and Clinton AME Zion Greenport; Rev. Dr. Peter J. Kelley and First Presbyterian Church of Southold; Rev. Dr. Faye Taylor and New Brunswick Theological Seminary.

Thank you to the congregation of Shinnecock Presbyterian Church, Southampton, and all my anonymous friends.

Thank you to Christen Kincaid and the team at Finishing Line Press for your expertise, patience and commitment.

Susan M. G. Dingle (formerly known as Susan Grathwohl) received an MA in Creative Writing from the University of Illinois at Chicago. Between 1971-1976, her poetry was published in *APR*, the *Ohio Review*, *Partisan Review*, *Feminist Studies* and elsewhere, and in *For Neruda, For Chile*, an anthology edited by Walter Lowenfels (Beacon Press, 1976). In 2013, she resumed publication as Susan Dingle in *The Poetry of Well-Being*, with Maggie Bloomfield and Nina Yavel. Her poems have since appeared in *Fifth Wednesday Journal*, and several anthologies with Local Gems. She has featured at readings throughout Long Island. In 2014, with Robert A. "Bubbie" Brown, Susan started and hosted Poetry Street at the Blue Duck Bakery Café in Riverhead. In 2016, in collaboration with Maggie Bloomfield, she wrote, produced and performed *Break Out!*, a two-woman show about recovery told in poetry, at the Southampton Cultural Center in 2016, and at the East End Fringe Festival in Riverhead in 2017. In 2017 Susan received the Rev. Dr. Martin Luther King Meritorious Award from First Baptist Church of Riverhead. She is currently in the M.Div. Program at New Brunswick Theological Seminary, and preaches throughout Long Island, a testimony to God's amazing grace. *Parting Gifts*, her first collection, was published by Local Gems in 2019. See also *www.poetrystreetontheroad.com* and *www.susandingle.com*.

www.ingramcontent.com/pod-product-compliance
Lightning Source LLC
LaVergne TN
LVHW041601070426
835507LV00011B/1239